# C

# Illustrations

£2.00

Nov
HISB

Why Everyone Should Read the

# Rubaiyat

Omar Khayyam and Edward Fitzgerald

Edited by Paulin Prifti

Illustrations by Silvia Gallani

**PAUL SMITH PUBLISHING**
London

Published by Paul Smith Publishing London

Published in this paperback edition in 2015

Copyright © Paul Smith Publishing 2014

Text and Notes © Paulin Prifti 2014

Illustrations Silvia Gallani

Cover design Francesca Crisafulli

ISBN 978-0-9927170-3-2

Paul Smith Publishing

www.paulsmithpublishing.co.uk

To Edward FitzGerald

*Within the Tavern caught Better than in the Temple lost outright*

# How the Rubaiyat was Found

One afternoon in early spring 1861 Dante Gabriel Rossetti, an English painter and poet, was walking down Charing Cross Road in London looking at various bookshops. Then, the same as now, booksellers placed tables and baskets by the door with books for sale at discounted prices.

Rossetti stopped at and searched a basket full of books priced at one penny each. He picked up a book called, *"Rubaiyat of Omar Khayyám the Astronomer-Poet of Persia, Translated into English Verse"*. Curious at the unusual title, he started reading and couldn't stop, standing there reading till he finished the entire book. The same evening we went to see a group of friends, the poet Swinburne amongst them, and read the Rubaiyat to them with excitement. It was an instant hit.

In a short time the poem became famous, and from a book that was a total failure it turned into the most read poem in the English language. It was used throughout the Oxford Dictionary of quotations, and it became even more popular in the USA. First edition copies became sought after.

Omar Khayyám has created one of the most beautiful poems in existence, yet, it would have been unknown without Edward FitzGerald. It was his translation that made the Rubaiyat known throughout the world. It has been published hundreds of times and translated into almost every living language. It is one of the most read poems of all time. There have been many translations and adaptations by other writers, but none surpasses the version created by Edward FitzGerald.

The story has it that when Rossetti and Swinburne went back to the bookseller one day later to buy more copies of the book, the owner had raised the price to two pence. Rossetti found the price raise so high he had an argument with the stall-keeper. A few days later the price went up to four pence, then a guinea and soon all of the 210 available copies were gone.

# What is the Rubaiyat?

The Rubaiyat is a collection of individual poems called quatrains, each of which is made of four lines. Quatrains are a regular form for writing poetry in the Persian language.

Each quatrain is a separate poem and can fully stand on its own. It follows the expression of one topic or a single thought from the beginning to the end. It's similar to a sonnet in the English language, but in four lines instead of fourteen. Normally, the first, the second and the fourth lines rhyme, not the third.

Though close to 5000 quatrains of the Rubaiyat exist today, Omar Khayyám wrote between 250 and 300. The rest were written and added in his name after his death. One of the first known selections of some of his quatrains appeared in a compilation put together by Sheik Najmuddin Razi 103 after the poet's death.

Edward FitzGerald translated a total of 110 quatrains revised in five editions: 75 quatrains in the first edition; 110 in the second; and the third, the fourth, and the fifth had 101 quatrains each. While quatrain in Persian are in no particular order, FitzGerald grouped them and put them in an order resembling life's cycle; there's a beginning, middle and an end.

Some say Omar Khayyám wrote the Rubaiyat to express freely and give shape to his own thoughts, beliefs and concerns. Whatever the reason he wrote them for, the Rubaiyat are as beautiful and fresh now as in the day they were written.

Rubaiyat is a poem about life, its simple pleasures and everyday hopes and fears, and the finality of death. Life is short and no one knows what comes after; make the most of it.

# Who was Omar Khayyám?

Omar Khayyám was born between 1046 and 1048 in Nishapur city, Khorasan, Iran. He was one of the most accomplished scientists of his time. He studied philosophy, theology, history, medicine, physics, mathematics and astronomy. He lived at a time of unparalleled freedom of thought and scientific discovery throughout the Arab world, a time Europe was deep into the Dark Ages.

He wrote many works on philosophy and science of which not many have survived. Amongst the surviving are his *'Algebra'*, which was published in 1851 by von Woepke in Paris, and *'Metaphysical Notes'*, published in French in 1906 by Christiansen in *Le Monde Oriental*.

Khayyám worked on and reformed the solar calendar in 1074, still in use in Iran today. When I mentioned to a British-Iranian Londoner I was preparing a book on Khayyám's Rubaiyat, the first thing he talked about was Khayyám's calendar. Khayyám's calendar is considered to be as accurate as the Gregorian calendar.

There are not many details available about Omar Khayyám's life, and those that exist are often contradictory. It's unlikely he became a close school friend and made a pact with both the Great Vezir Nizam al Mulk and Haddan Sabahu, whom the Crusaders nicknamed the Old Man of the Mountains. Also, it's not true he lead a happy and comfortable life. Far from it, Khayyám went through many hardships.

Omar Khayyám, as a poet, has been popular in his country, Iran, for a long time. The earliest reference to Khayyám as a poet dates around 60 years after his death. However, it was FitzGerald's translation of the Rubaiyat that made both Khayyám and his poem hugely famous in Iran and worldwide.

Omar Khayyám died in 1213 in Nishapur of Khorasan, where he is buried. Rose bushes were planted by his grave according to his last wishes. He rests in the Khayyám Garden at the Imamzadeh Mahruq, a shrine, built for him in 1301. People from all over the world go and visit his grave.

# Who was Edward FitzGerald?

Edward FitzGerald was born in Woodbridge, Suffolk, England, on 31 March 1809 in a wealthy Anglo-Irish family.

FitzGerald wrote other works, however, the Rubaiyat is what he is famous for. He was introduced to the Rubaiyat in March 1856 by his close friend, Edward Cowell. Shortly before leaving for India, while going through a batch of old and forgotten manuscripts in the Bodleian Library in Oxford, Cowell came across a set of 158 Persian quatrains by Omar Khayyám, dated 1460. He gave FitzGerald a copy of the original.

FitzGerald was fascinated by the Rubaiyat and started working on it; he first translated the quatrains in Latin, then English. In January 1858 FitzGerald sent the poem to a London magazine, *Fraser's*, and not hearing any news from them for almost a year he decided to publish it himself. In April 1859 he ordered 250 copies in a twenty-four-page pamphlet form, kept 40 for friends and family and gave the rest to the publisher. No one bought it.

FitzGerald kept working on the poem all the time; he wanted to improve and perfect it. After the first edition he produced three revised editions. He published all four anonymously and refused the publisher's suggestion to include illustrations. There was one more edition, the fifth and last, published after his death.

After FitzGerald's death a friend of his, William Wright, found hidden in a tin box a draft of the fourth edition in which FitzGerald had made a few notes and changes. The fifth edition was published in 1889 as part of *Letters and Literary Remains of Edward FitzGerald* and it revealed for the first time Edward FitzGerald as the translator of the poem.

Edward FitzGerald died on 14 June 1883 at the age of 74, and is buried in a small and peaceful churchyard at St Michael's Church, in Boulge Park in Norfolk, England. A rose tree stands by his grave which originated from the rose bushes of Omar Khayyám's grave. It was a traveller, William Simpson, who after visiting Omar's grave in Nishapur brought back a few seeds in 1884. He planted them in Kew Gardens first, luckily two bore fruit, and then at FitzGerald's grave in Boulge in October 1893.

FitzGerald has been accused of changing and making a mockery of the real poem, of putting words into it Omar Khayyám didn't write. Even today, more than one and a half centuries later, scholars and the literary world still debate about this. Does it matter? The Rubaiyat is one of the most beautiful poems ever written; timeless and borderless.

This publication represents the first edition of the Rubaiyat with new illustrations by S. Gallani.

Enjoy.

# The Rubaiyat

Illustration 1

*Awake the Stone that puts the Stars to Flight*

**1**

AWAKE! for Morning in the Bowl of Night
Has flung the Stone that puts the Stars to Flight:
And Lo! the Hunter of the East has caught
The Sultan's Turret in a Noose of Light.

**2**

Dreaming when Dawn's Left Hand was in the Sky,
I heard a Voice within the Tavern cry,
"Awake, my Little ones, and fill the Cup
Before Life's Liquor in its Cup be dry."

**3**

And, as the Cock crew, those who stood before
The Tavern shouted—"Open then the Door!
You know how little while we have to stay,
And, once departed, may return no more."

**4**

Now the New Year reviving old Desires,
The thoughtful Soul to Solitude retires,
Where the WHITE HAND of Moses on the Bough
Puts out, and Jesus from the Ground suspires.

**5**

Iram indeed is gone with all its Rose,
And Jamshyd's Sev'n-ring'd Cup where no one
knows;
But still the Vine her ancient Ruby yields,
And still a Garden by the Water blows.

# Illustration 2

*A Flask of Wine, a Book of Verse-singing in the Wilderness*

**6**

And David's Lips are lock't; but in divine
High piping Pehlevi, with "Wine! Wine! Wine!
*Red* Wine!"-the Nightingale cries to the Rose
That yellow Cheek of hers to incarnadine.

**7**

Come, fill the Cup, and in the Fire of Spring
The Winter Garment of Repentance fling:
The Bird of Time has but a little way
To fly-and Lo! the Bird is on the Wing.

**8**

And look-a thousand Blossoms with the Day
Woke-and a thousand scatter'd into Clay:
And this first Summer Month that brings the Rose
Shall take Jamshyd and Kaikobad away.

**9**

But come with old Khayyam, and leave the Lot
Of Kaikobad and Kaikhosru forgot:
Let Rustum lay about him as he will,
Or Hatim Tai cry Supper-heed them not.

**10**

With me along some Strip of Herbage strown
That just divides the desert from the sown,
Where name of Slave and Sultan scarce is known,
And pity Sultan Mahmud on his Throne.

# Illustration 3

*My Purse and its Treasure into the World I blow*

**11**

Here with a Loaf of Bread beneath the Bough,
A Flask of Wine, a Book of Verse-and Thou
Beside me singing in the Wilderness-
And Wilderness is Paradise enow.

**12**

"How sweet is mortal Sovranty!"-think some:
Others-"How blest the Paradise to come!"
Ah, take the Cash in hand and waive the Rest;
Oh, the brave Music of a *distant* Drum!

**13**

Look to the Rose that blows about us-"Lo,
Laughing," she says, "into the World I blow:
At once the silken Tassel of my Purse
Tear, and its Treasure on the Garden throw."

**14**

The Worldly Hope men set their Hearts upon
Turns Ashes-or it prospers; and anon,
Like Snow upon the Desert's dusty Face
Lighting a little Hour or two-is gone.

**15**

And those who husbanded the Golden Grain,
And those who flung it to the Winds like Rain,
Alike to no such aureate Earth are turn'd
As, buried once, Men want dug up again.

Illustration 4

*The Courts the Lion and the Lizard gloried and drank deep*

**16**

Think, in this batter'd Caravanserai
Whose Doorways are alternate Night and Day,
How Sultan after Sultan with his Pomp
Abode his Hour or two and went his way.

**17**

They say the Lion and the Lizard keep
The Courts where Jamshyd gloried and drank deep:
And Bahram, that great Hunter-the Wild Ass
Stamps o'er his Head, and he lies fast asleep.

**18**

I sometimes think that never blows so red
The Rose as where some buried Caesar bled;
That every Hyacinth the Garden wears
Dropt in its Lap from some once lovely Head.

**19**

And this delightful Herb whose tender Green
Fledges the River's Lip on which we lean-
Ah, lean upon it lightly! for who knows
From what once lovely Lip it springs unseen!

**20**

Ah! my Beloved, fill the Cup that clears
TO-DAY of past Regrets and future Fears-
*To-morrow*?-Why, To-morrow I may be
Myself with Yesterday's Sev'n Thousand Years.

Illustration 5

*The River's Lip on which we lean upon*

**21**

Lo! some we loved, the loveliest and the best
That Time and Fate of all their Vintage prest,
Have drunk their Cup a Round or two before,
And one by one crept silently to Rest.

**22**

And we, that now make merry in the Room
They left, and Summer dresses in new Bloom,
Ourselves must we beneath the Couch of Earth
Descend, ourselves to make a Couch-for whom?

**23**

Ah, make the most of what we yet may spend,
Before we too into the Dust Descend;
Dust into Dust, and under Dust, to lie,
Sans Wine, sans Song, sans Singer and-sans End!

**24**

Alike for those who for TO-DAY prepare,
And those that after a TO-MORROW stare,
A Muezzin from the Tower of Darkness cries,
"Fools! your Reward is neither Here nor There!"

**25**

Why, all the Saints and Sages who discuss'd
Of the Two Worlds so learnedly, are thrust
Like foolish Prophets forth; their Words to Scorn
Are scatter'd, and their Mouths are stopt with Dust.

**26**

Oh, come with old Khayyam, and leave the Wise
To talk; one thing is certain, that Life flies;
One thing is certain, and the Rest is Lies;
The Flower that once has blown for ever dies.

**27**

Myself when young did eagerly frequent
Doctor and Saint, and heard great Argument
About it and about; but evermore
Came out by the same Door as in I went.

**28**

With them the Seed of Wisdom did I sow,
And with my own hand labour'd it to grow:
And this was all the Harvest that I reap'd-
"I came like Water and like Wind I go."

**29**

Into this Universe, and *why* not knowing,
Nor *whence*, like Water willy-nilly flowing:
And out of it, as Wind along the Waste,
I know not *whither*, willy-nilly blowing.

**30**

What, without asking, hither hurried *whence*?
And, without asking, *whither* hurried hence!
Another and another Cup to drown
The Memory of this Impertinence!

**31**

Up from Earth's Centre through the seventh Gate
I rose, and on the Throne of Saturn sate,
And many Knots unravel'd by the Road;
But not the Knot of Human Death and Fate.

**32**

There was a Door to which I found no Key:
There was a Veil past which I could not see:
Some little Talk awhile of ME and THEE
There seemed-and then no more of THEE and ME.

**33**

Then to the rolling Heav'n itself I cried,
Asking, "What Lamp had Destiny to guide
Her little Children stumbling in the Dark?"
And-"A blind understanding!" Heav'n replied.

**34**

Then to this earthen Bowl did I adjourn
My Lip the secret Well of Life to learn:
And Lip to Lip it murmur'd-"While you live
Drink!-for once dead you never shall return."

**35**

I think the Vessel, that with fugitive
Articulation answer'd, once did live,
And merry-make; and the cold Lip I kiss'd
How many Kisses might it take-and give!

Illustration 6

*Beneath the Couch of Earth Descend-for whom?*

**36**

For in the Market-place, one Dusk of Day,
I watch'd the Potter thumping his wet Clay:
And with its all obliterated Tongue
It murmur'd-"Gently, Brother, gently pray!"

**37**

Ah, fill the Cup:-what boots it to repeat
How Time is slipping underneath our Feet:
Unborn TO-MORROW and dead YESTERDAY,
Why fret about them if TO-DAY be sweet!

**38**

One Moment in Annihilation's Waste,
One moment, of the Well of Life to taste-
The Stars are setting and the Caravan
Starts for the Dawn of Nothing-Oh, make haste!

**39**

How long, how long, in infinite Pursuit
Of This and That endeavour and dispute?
Better be merry with the fruitful Grape
Than sadden after none, or bitter, Fruit.

**40**

You know, my Friends, how long since in my House
For a new Marriage I did make Carouse:
Divorced old barren Reason from my Bed,
And took the Daughter of the Vine to Spouse.

Illustration 7

*I rose and on the Throne of Saturn sate*

**41**

For "IS" and "IS-NOT" though *with* Rule and Line,
And, "UP-AND-DOWN" *without*, I could define,
 I yet in all I only cared to know,
Was never deep in anything but-Wine.

**42**

And lately, by the Tavern Door agape,
Came stealing through the Dusk an Angel Shape
 Bearing a vessel on his Shoulder; and
He bid me taste of it; and 'twas-the Grape!

**43**

The Grape that can with Logic absolute
The Two-and-Seventy jarring Sects confute:
 The subtle Alchemist that in a Trice
Life's leaden Metal into Gold transmute.

**44**

The mighty Mahmud, the victorious Lord,
That all the misbelieving and black Horde
 Of Fears and Sorrows that infest the Soul
Scatters and slays with his enchanted Sword.

**45**

But leave the Wise to wrangle, and with me
The Quarrel of the Universe let be:
 And in some corner of the Hubbub coucht,
Make Game of that which makes as much of Thee.

# Illustration 8

*The Caravan Starts for the Dawn of Nothing*

**46**

For in and out, above, about, below,
'Tis nothing but a Magic Shadow-show,
Play'd in a Box whose Candle is the Sun,
Round which we Phantom Figures come and go.

**47**

And if the Wine you drink, the Lip you press,
End in the Nothing all Things end in-Yes-
Then fancy while Thou art, Thou art but what
Thou shalt be-Nothing-Thou shalt not be less.

**48**

While the Rose blows along the River Brink,
With old Khayyam the Ruby Vintage drink:
And when the Angel with his darker Draught
Draws up to thee-take that, and do not shrink.

**49**

'Tis all a Chequer-board of Nights and Days
Where Destiny with Men for Pieces plays:
Hither and thither moves, and mates, and slays,
And one by one back in the Closet lays.

**50**

The Ball no Question makes of Ayes and Noes,
But Right or Left, as strikes the Player goes;
And He that toss'd Thee down into the Field,
*He* knows about it all-HE knows-HE knows!

**51**

The Moving Finger writes; and, having writ,
Moves on: nor all thy Piety nor Wit
Shall lure it back to cancel half a Line,
Nor all thy Tears wash out a Word of it.

**52**

And that inverted Bowl we call The Sky,
Whereunder crawling coop't we live and die,
Lift not thy hands to *It* for help-for It
Rolls impotently on as Thou or I.

**53**

With Earth's first Clay They did the Last Man's
knead.
And then of the Last Harvest sow'd the Seed:
Yea, the first Morning of Creation wrote
What the Last Dawn of Reckoning shall read.

**54**

I tell Thee this-When, starting from the Goal,
Over the shoulders of the flaming Foal
Of Heav'n Parwin and Mushtara they flung,
In my predestin'd Plot of Dust and Soul

**55**

The Vine had struck a Fibre; which about
It clings my Being-let the Sufi flout;
Of my Base Metal may be filed a Key,
That shall unlock the Door he howls without.

Illustration 9

*An Angel Shape Came stealing through the Tavern Door*

**56**

And this I know: whether the one True Light,
Kindle to Love, or Wrath-consume me quite,
One Glimpse of It within the Tavern caught
Better than in the Temple lost outright.

**57**

Oh, Thou, who didst with Pitfall and with Gin
Beset the Road I was to wander in,
Thou wilt not with Predestination round
Enmesh me, and impute my Fall to Sin?

**58**

Oh, Thou, who Man of baser Earth didst make,
And who with Eden didst devise the Snake;
For all the Sin wherewith the Face of Man
Is blacken'd, Man's Forgiveness give-and take!

**59**

Listen again. One Evening at the Close
Of Ramazan, ere the better Moon arose,
In that old Potter's Shop I stood alone
With the clay Population round in Rows.

**60**

And, strange to tell, among that Earthen Lot
Some could articulate, while others not:
And suddenly one more impatient cried-
"Who *is* the Potter, pray, and who the Pot?"

Illustration 10

*A Magic Shadow-show We Phantom Figures come and go*

**61**

Then said another-"Surely not in vain
My substance from the common Earth was ta'en,
That He who subtly wrought me into Shape
Should stamp me back to common Earth again."

**62**

Another said-"Why, ne'er a peevish Boy,
Would break the Bowl from which he drank in Joy;
Shall He that *made* the Vessel in pure Love
And Fancy, in an after Rage destroy?"

**63**

None answer'd this; but after Silence spake
A Vessel of a more ungainly Make:
"They sneer at me for leaning all awry;
What! did the Hand then of the Potter shake?"

**64**

Said one-"Folks of a surly Tapster tell,
And daub his Visage with the Smoke of Hell;
They talk of some strict Testing of us-Pish!
He's a Good Fellow, and 'twill all be well."

**65**

Then said another with a long-drawn Sigh,
"My Clay with long oblivion is gone dry:
But, fill me with the old familiar Juice,
Methinks I might recover by-and-bye!"

**66**

So while the Vessels one by one were speaking,
One spied the little Crescent all were seeking:
And then they jogg'd each other, "Brother! Brother!
Hark to the Porter's Shoulder-knot a-creaking!"

**67**

Ah, with the Grape my fading Life provide,
And wash my Body whence the life has died,
And in a Winding sheet of Vine leaf wrapt,
So bury me by some sweet Garden side.

**68**

That ev'n my buried Ashes such a Snare
Of Perfume shall fling up into the Air,
As not a True Believer passing by
But shall be overtaken unaware.

**69**

Indeed the Idols I have loved so long
Have done my Credit in Men's Eye much wrong:
Have drown'd my Honour in a shallow Cup,
And sold my Reputation for a Song.

**70**

Indeed, indeed, Repentance oft before
I swore-but was I sober when I swore?
And then and then came Spring, and Rose-in-hand
My thread-bare Penitence apieces tore.

Illustration 11

*A Chequer-board Where Destiny with Men for Pieces plays*

**71**

And much as Wine has play'd the Infidel,
And robb'd me of my Robe of Honour-well,
I often wonder what the Vintners buy
One half so precious as the Goods they sell.

**72**

Alas, that Spring should vanish with the Rose!
That Youth's sweet-scented Manuscript should close!
The Nightingale that in the Branches sang,
Ah, whence, and whither flown again, who knows!

**73**

Ah Love! could thou and I with Fate conspire
To grasp this sorry Scheme of Things entire,
Would not we shatter it to bits-and then
Re-mould it nearer to the Heart's Desire!

Illustration 12

*The Moon of Heav'n is rising once again*

**74**

Ah, Moon of my Delight who know'st no wane,
The Moon of Heav'n is rising once again:
How oft hereafter rising shall she look
Through this same Garden after me-in vain!

**75**

And when Thyself with shining Foot shall pass
Among the Guests Star-scatter'd on the Grass,
And in Thy joyous Errand reach the Spot
Where I made one-turn down an empty Glass!

TAMAM SHUD

15006183R10026

Printed in Great Britain
by Amazon.co.uk, Ltd.,
Marston Gate.